CAMBRIDGE
UNIVERSITY PRESS

CAMBRIDGE ENGLISH
Language Assessment
Part of the University of Cambridge

CAMBRIDGE

T0343453

STORYFUN 2

STUDENT'S BOOK

with Online Activities
and Home Fun Booklet 2

Second edition

Karen Saxby

Cambridge University Press
www.cambridge.org/elt

Cambridge Assessment English
www.cambridgeenglish.org

Information on this title: www.cambridge.org/9781316617021

© Cambridge University Press & Assessment 2017

First published 2011
Second edition 2017

40 39 38 37 36 35 34 33 32 31 30 29 28 27 26

Printed in Poland by Opolgraf

A catalogue record for this publication is available from the British Library

ISBN 978-1-316-61702-1 Student's Book with online activities and Home Fun booklet
ISBN 978-1-316-61709-0 Teacher's Book with Audio
ISBN 978-1-316-61713-7 Presentation Plus

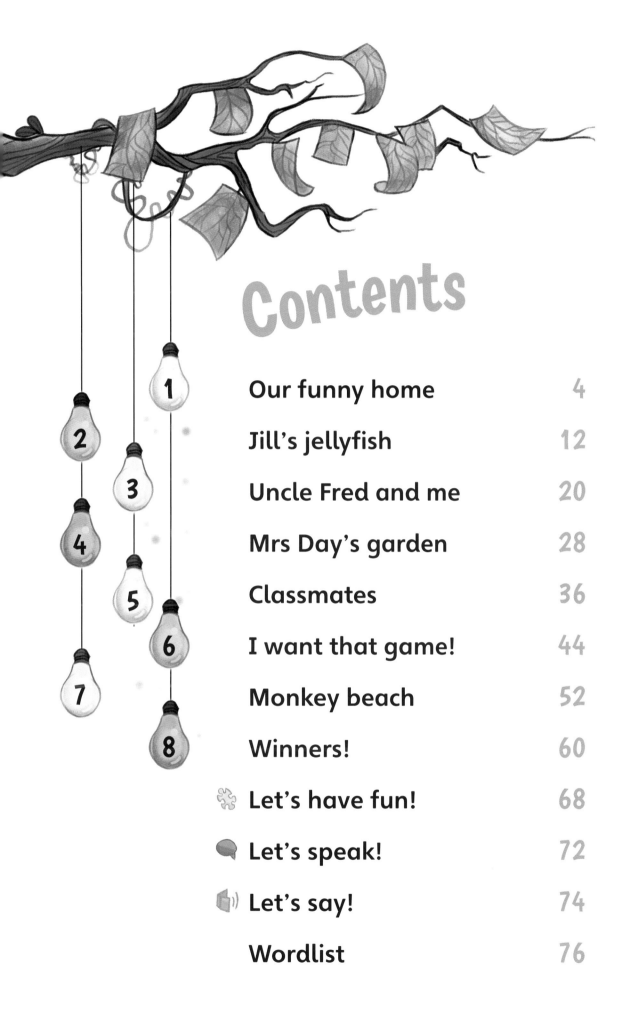

Contents

1   Our funny home   4

2   Jill's jellyfish   12

3   Uncle Fred and me   20

4   Mrs Day's garden   28

5   Classmates   36

6   I want that game!   44

7   Monkey beach   52

8   Winners!   60

Let's have fun!   68

Let's speak!   72

Let's say!   74

Wordlist   76

Our funny home

1

Our home is really funny.

The window is under the cupboard.

Our radio is in Mum's old hat.

There are three chairs in front of those flowers

and ten oranges next to the cat ...

in our **kitchen**!

My grandma's sleeping in the bath again!
Look! She's behind her funny old door.
Five ducks are enjoying the water and
can you see those four boats on the floor ...

in our **bathroom**?

The TV is between two big bookcases.

My pet lizard lives under it. Oh ...

there are nine balloons on Dad's armchair today.

And where is our baby hippo?

In our **living room**!

Two clocks are behind that painting of frogs.

My football is here! It's not in our hall.

Grandpa's teeth are on our big table again.

And can you see the tree on the wall ...

in our **dining room**?

My lamp is in front of six boxes.

There are 11 new books on my head.

Our green snake sleeps on that computer

and there are 12 shoes under my bed ...

in my **bedroom**!

Our home is old and we have lots of pets.

Mum says, 'It's like a zoo!'

But I love my family and I love my home!

Would you like to live here too?

Our funny home

A Draw lines.

1 I go to bed and sleep in my …   **a** bathroom.

2 I clean my face and hands in our …   **b** kitchen.

3 I make cakes with my mother in our …   **c** bedroom.

4 I eat with my family in our …   **d** living room.

5 I sit on the sofa and watch TV in our … **e** hall.

6 I come home and walk into our …   **f** dining room.

B Find the words and write.

lizardelevenhatgreenflowersgrandmatree

1 Where is the radio?   in Mum's ....hat....

2 Who is in the bath?   ....

3 What is on the dining room wall?   a ....

4 Which animal is under the TV?   a ....

5 How many books are on the boy's head? ....

6 What colour is the snake?   ....

C Which boy is correct? Read and tick (✔) the box.

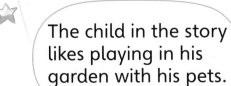

The child in the story likes playing in his garden with his pets.

The child in the story loves his family. He loves his home too.

The child in the story likes going to the zoo. He loves animals.

1  SAM ☐

2  MATT ☐

3  TOM ☐

D Look at the pictures. Look at the letters. Write the words.

Example

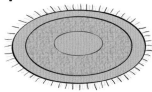 r u g

Questions

1  _ _ _

2   _ _ _ _

3  _ _ _ _

4   _ _ _ _ _ _

5  _ _ _ _ _ _ _ _

E ▶ Listen and write the numbers.

03

I've got ...12... socks and .... shoes.
Which ones can I wear? I can't choose!

I've got .... games and .... toys.
Who can I play with? One of those boys?

I've got .... pencils and .... pens.
Whose book can I write in? Jill's or Ben's?

Now I've got .... sweets and .... fries.
What can I eat? I know! Those two pies!

F Look and read. Write *yes* or *no*.

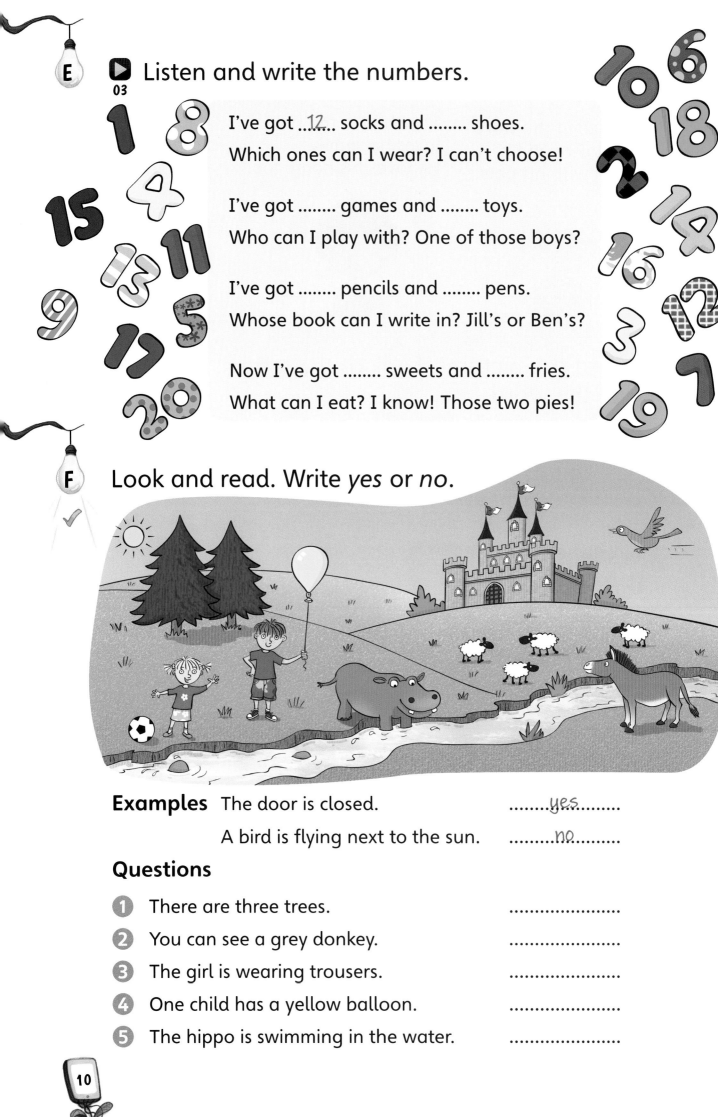

Examples   The door is closed.   ....yes.........

A bird is flying next to the sun.   ....no.........

Questions

1   There are three trees.   ....

2   You can see a grey donkey.   ....

3   The girl is wearing trousers.   ....

4   One child has a yellow balloon.   ....

5   The hippo is swimming in the water.   ....

G ▶ Listen and tick (✔) the box.

Example Which is Mark's flat?   **1** Where are Anna's new pens?

A ✔   B ☐   C ☐   A ☐   B ☐   C ☐

2 Who is Grace phoning now?   **3** What is in the baby's bath?

A ☐   B ☐   C ☐   A ☐   B ☐   C ☐

4 Where is the cat?   **5** Which is Grandmother's T-shirt?

A ☐   B ☐   C ☐   A ☐   B ☐   C ☐

H Choose the words for you.

1 I live in a  **house / flat / piano / boat.**

2 There is a **bed / elephant / desk / armchair** in my bedroom.

3 There are **flowers / lamps / games / rugs** in our living room.

4 There is a **mirror / crocodile / mat / bath** in our bathroom.

p.
68

p.
72

11

Jill's jellyfish

Nick, Sue and Ben are friends. They're playing a game. Nick is choosing an animal and his friends, Sue and Ben, are asking questions.

'How many legs have you got?' asks Sue. 'Four!' says Nick.

'What colour are you?' asks Ben. 'One of my colours is white,' says Nick. Ben's little sister, Jill, wants to play too.

'Can I try, please?' she asks. 'You're a cow!'

'No, Jill.'

'Well, you're a horse or a polar bear!'

'No, Jill.'

'Then you're a zebra!' says Ben.

'That's right!' says Nick. 'Now you choose an animal, Ben.'

'Which food do you eat?' asks Sue.

'Meat.'

'Where do you live?' asks Nick.

'In or next to water,' says Ben.

Can I try again?

'You're a frog!'

'No, Jill.'

'Well, you're a lizard or a hippo!'

'No, Jill.'

'Then you're a crocodile,' says Sue.

'Yes, Sue! Now you!' says Ben.

'Have you got legs?' asks Nick.

'Yes, and one of my colours is orange,' says Sue.

'I know!' says Jill. 'You're a giraffe, a tiger or a chicken!'

'No, Jill. Sorry!'

'Then you're a bee,' says Nick.

'Fantastic! OK. You can choose now, Jill,' says Ben.

'Hooray!' says Jill.

'What colour are you?' asks Sue.

'I'm lots of colours.'

'Are you big or small?' asks Ben.

'I'm big OR small.'

'Are you beautiful or ugly?' asks Ben.

'I'm beautiful.'

'Whose favourite animal are you?' asks Sue.

'Mine! I love them!' says Jill. 'It's MY favourite animal!'

'Oh dear, we don't know the answer!' say Ben, Nick and Sue.

'What animal are you?'

'I'm a Jelly, Jilly, Jellyfish,' sings Jill.

'Well done, Jelly, Jilly, Jellyfish!' say Ben, Nick and Sue.

15

2

Jill's jellyfish

A Write the words in the correct box.

~~bee~~ **tiger** chicken giraffe zebra lizard

small **animals**	**big** animals
.........bee.........	....
....	....
....	....

B Look and read. Choose the correct word.

1. Jill is Ben's little (sister) / **cousin** / **friend**.
2. **Nick** / **Ben** / **Sue** chooses a zebra in the game.
3. Jill says, 'Can I **fly** / **start** / **try** again?'
4. Ben's animal is a **crocodile** / **hippo** / **horse**.
5. One of the colours of Sue's animal is **orange** / **white** / **grey**.
6. Jill's animal is **ugly** / **young** / **beautiful**.

C What can Ben say about Jill? Tick (✔) the correct answe

1. She asks a lot of really funny questions. ☐
2. She tries and tries and finds the answer. ☐
3. She listens and likes learning new things. ☐

D Look and read. Put a tick (✔) or a cross (✘) in the box.

Examples

   This is a giraffe. ✔

   These are teddy bears. ✘

Questions

①    This is a woman. ☐

②    This is a mouth. ☐

③    This is meat. ☐

④    These are bees. ☐

⑤    This is a tail. ☐

E Look and read. Write the correct question word.

~~What~~   How many   Where   What   Whose   Who

① ....What....... colour is your dog?   It is brown.

② .... are you talking to?   My brother.

③ .... is your pet mouse?   In a box.

④ .... is your donkey doing?   It is having lunch.

⑤ .... chickens have you got?   We have got 16.

⑥ .... cat is this?   It is Sue's cat.

F Look at the pictures and read the questions.
Write one-word answers.

Examples

What is the bear doing?   ....~~sleeping~~....

Where is the bird?   in the ......~~tree~~........

Questions

1 How many children can you see?   ....

2 What is the girl holding?   some ....

3 What is the bird doing?   ....

4 What is the girl giving to the bear?   an ....

5 Where is the bird now?   on the bear's ....

G Listen to your teacher and point. Then draw lines.

H Listen and sing the song.
06

Jellyfish! Look, jellyfish!
And sandfish, happy sandfish
Swim, swim, swim
in the sea!

Goatfish! Look, goatfish!
And cowfish, funny cowfish
Live in the water,
not in a tree!

Catfish! Look, catfish!
And dogfish, scary dogfish!
Swim, swim, swim
in the sea!

Sunfish! Look, sunfish!
And starfish, little starfish
Love being in the water,
like you and me!

p. 68

p. 72

Uncle Fred and me

My uncle Fred likes going to the park and running with his friends.

My uncle Fred likes fishing in the lake, watching hockey on TV and eating chocolate cake!
'Wow! What a big fish!
Oh no!
What an old boot!'
says Uncle Fred.

My uncle Fred loves
walking with his ducks
and singing in the rain.

My uncle Fred loves
playing his guitar,
wearing very silly clothes and
taking photos of his car!
'What a beautiful yellow car!
I love my car!'
says Uncle Fred.

I love jumping, one, two, three,
and reading scary stories in this tree.

I like watching happy little birds and
I love spelling very long words.
Alphabet! What a long word!

Uncle Fred and I love wearing funny socks
and sitting on these rocks.

We love finding big white shells and
swimming in the sea.
I love my uncle Fred and my uncle Fred loves me!

Uncle Fred and me

A Write the words in the correct box.

~~jumping~~ running **spelling** watching TV
taking photos **reading** fishing
riding a bike singing

I like …

jumping

Uncle Fred likes …

B Look and read. Choose the correct word.

1. Uncle Fred loves his **guitar** / **jeans**.
2. Uncle Fred likes **football** / **hockey**.
3. Uncle Fred likes **chocolate cake** / **apple pie**.
4. Uncle Fred loves his **yellow** / **orange** car.
5. Lucy likes her **kite** / **ball**.
6. Lucy likes her **camera** / **bike**.
7. Lucy and Uncle Fred love big white **flowers** / **shells**.

C Write and draw lines.

1 Uncle Fred 😊 ......likes....... running.

2 He ❤ ......loves....... playing his guitar.

3 He 😊 .... watching hockey on TV.

4 He ❤ .... singing in the rain.

5 He ❤ .... taking photos of his car.

6 He 😊 .... fishing in the lake.

7 He ❤ .... wearing silly clothes.

What about you?

I love .... in the morning, I love

.... in the afternoon and I love

.... in the evening.

I love doing this!

D Write and draw.

cool   silly   beautiful   scary   funny   big   fantastic   good

1

What a ...funny... duck!

2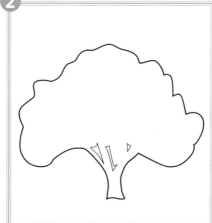

What a .... tree!

3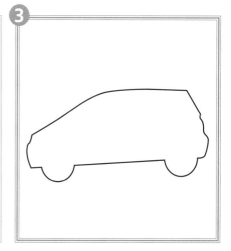

What a .... car!

E ▶ Listen and draw lines.
08

Pat	Alice	Eva	Dan

May   Hugo   Lucy

F Ask and answer.

Do you like singing?

No, I don't.

Yes, I do!

Do you like taking photos?

G Read. Choose a word from the box and write.

Lots of people like listening to music in the ......evening...... . Some like listening to it on their computers or ❶ .... Tim likes singing ❷ .... , too. He sings them in his bedroom. He likes singing in the ❸ .... , too! Tim has got a ❹ .... He loves playing it. He plays it in his music ❺ .... at school.

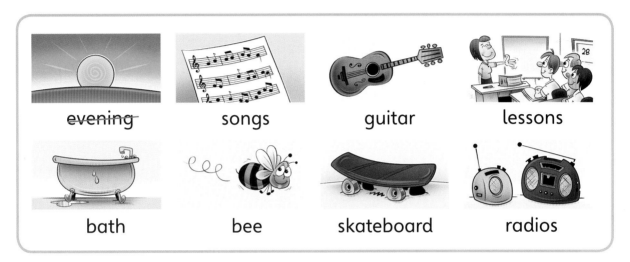

evening   songs   guitar   lessons

bath   bee   skateboard   radios

H ▶ Listen and colour.
09

p. 69

p. 72

Mrs Day's garden

4

Mr Gray is a farmer. There are cows, sheep, goats, ducks and chickens on his farm. There's a dog too!

Mrs Day lives next to Mr Gray's farm. There are potatoes, onions, beans, peas and two pear trees in her garden.

Mr Gray is going to the town now. He's going in his truck. Mrs Day is going to the shops. She's going on the bus.

Oh dear!

Mr Gray's farm gate is open.

Oh dear!

Mrs Day's garden gate is open too!

Look at the cows and sheep!

Look at the goats and ducks and chickens!

They're running and jumping

in Mrs Day's garden!

They're eating her potatoes and her onions and peas.

They're eating her beans and the pears in her trees.

They're wearing her hats and her T-shirts and shirts.

They're wearing her dresses and sweaters and skirts!

But look! Here's Mrs Day.

She's coming home from the shops.

Mr Gray's coming home too.

'I'm very angry!' says Mrs Day.

'Look at my clothes and look at my trees!'

'I'm very sorry!' says Mr Gray.

Would you like to
have dinner with me?

Mrs Day's garden

4

A Look, count and write.

........two........ cows

.... sheep

.... goats

.... onions

.... beans

.... potatoes

B Look and number the pictures.

C Look, read and write.

clothes animals bus ~~farm~~ truck

1. Mr Gray has got lots of animals on his ....farm........ .
2. Mr Gray drives his .... to town.
3. Mrs Day goes to town on a ....
4. The .... eat Mrs Day's potatoes, onions and peas.
5. They wear Mrs Day's .... Oh dear!

D Look and read. Say and answer.

Your animals are eating my flowers. I am very angry.

I'm very sorry. Would you like to have dinner with me?

1 Your pet frog is sitting on my new phone! I am not happy!

2 Your baby brother is drawing on my baseball cap. I am angry!

3 Your pet goat is eating my school bag! I am really angry now!

E 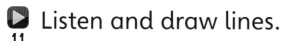 Listen and draw lines.
11

F Write and say.

For breakfast, I eat
....

For lunch, I eat
....

For dinner, I eat
....

G Look, read and write.

1. The brown cow is wearing a dirty blue ....skirt........ .
2. The duck is wearing a dirty green ....
3. The black sheep is wearing a dirty white ....
4. The chicken is wearing a dirty red and yellow ....
5. The grey goat is wearing a dirty pink ....
6. The black and white cow is wearing a dirty yellow ....

H ▶ Read the questions. Listen and write a name or a number.

12

Examples

What is the boy's name? ......Mark.......

How old is the boy? ....12..........

1. Where does Mark live? in .... Street
2. What is the name of Mark's dog? ....
3. How many chickens has Mr Gray got? ....
4. What is the name of Mark's favourite cow? ....
5. How many goats live on Mr Gray's farm? ....

34

I Look. Ask and answer.

1  **2**  **3**

> What is that boy doing?

> That boy is playing football!

4  **5**  **6**

J Look, listen and say.

   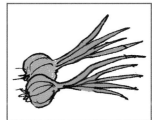

Now draw and write. Then ask and answer.

What is this?
What is the colour of this
.... ?
Do you like .... ?
What is your favourite
.... ?

> What is this?

> It is a ... .

p. 69

p. 72

Classmates

The children in Mr Bath's class are reading stories this morning.

They're reading about a jungle and a zoo.

The monster in Mr Bath's class isn't reading stories this morning.

It's painting suns and stars on Anna's shoe!

The children in Mr Bath's class are having their lunch now. They're eating fish and chips and peas and bread.

The monster from Mr Bath's classroom isn't having its lunch now. It's throwing paper planes at Sam and Fred!

The children in Mr Bath's class are doing lots of sports now.
They're playing soccer, tennis or baseball.
The monster from Mr Bath's classroom isn't doing sport now. It's drawing funny faces on the wall!

The children in Mr Bath's class are going home now.
They're getting their tablets and bags and books and pens.

The monster in Mr Bath's class isn't going home now.
It lives behind the door of classroom ten!

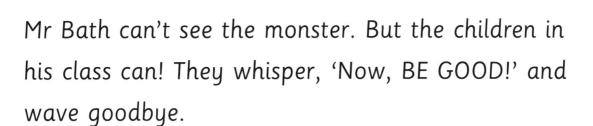

Mr Bath can't see the monster. But the children in his class can! They whisper, 'Now, BE GOOD!' and wave goodbye.

But the monster isn't listening. It's playing the piano! They love their friend, the monster.

So do I!

Classmates

A Read and write.

1. The monster likes playing the **p i a n o** with its funny hands.

2. The children in Anna's class are her **c _ _ ssm _ _ es**.

3. A **t _ _ _ _ t** is a small computer you can put in a school bag.

4. At school you can write on **p _ _ _ r** with a pencil or pen.

5. **T _ _ _ _ s** is a game two or four people play with a small ball.

B Look and read. Choose the correct word.

1. The name of Anna's teacher is **Mr** / **Mrs** Bath.

2. The children read about a **park** / **jungle**.

3. The monster paints Anna's **shoe** / **face**.

4. The children eat **meatballs** / **fish** for their lunch.

5. The monster draws funny faces on a **wall** / **tablet**.

6. The monster lives **behind** / **next to** the classroom door.

7. The teacher **can** / **can't** see the monster.

8. The monster plays the **guitar** / **piano**.

C ▶ Read the questions. Listen and write a name or
14   a number.

Examples

What is the monster's name?   ......Hobby......

How many words can the monster read?   ....9..........

① Where does the monster live?   .... School

② Which classroom is the monster in now?   ....

③ How many crayons has the monster got?   ....

④ Who gives chips to the monster?   ....

⑤ How many paints has the monster got?   ....

D Look, read and write.

| sleeping   eating   reading   drinking   isn't   singing |
| painting   painting writing   writing   drawing |

①

②

ⓐ Fred is ....drawing.... .

ⓑ The teacher is ....

ⓒ Anna is ....

ⓓ The monster is ....
a picture.

ⓐ Fred isn't drawing. He is ....sleeping.... .

ⓑ The teacher .... singing.
He is .... juice.

ⓒ Anna isn't ....
She is..................... an apple.

ⓓ The monster isn't ....
a picture.

It is .... a funny story.

E Read. Choose a word from the box and write.

Many homes have dining rooms. Anna's ......*school*...... has a dining room too. The children in Anna's class don't read their English ❶ .... or look at their tablets in their dining room. They sit on green ❷ .... , put their food on the ❸ .... and talk and eat their lunch there. Today, they're eating fish and ❹ .... in their dining room. They're drinking orange ❺ .... too.

~~school~~	chairs	books	pen
juice	table	bag	chips

F Look and write. Then ask and answer.

~~reading~~   painting   listening to music   counting
drawing animals   colouring   spelling long words   making a poster

❶ ....*reading*.... ❷ .... ❸ .... ❹ ....

❺ .... ❻ .... ❼ .... ❽ ....

What do you like doing?

I love painting!

So do I!

I don't!

G  Listen and tick (✔) the box.

15

1 What is the monster playing?

A ☐

B ☐

C ☐

2 What is in the monster's bag?

A ☐

B ☐

C ☐

H Look. Ask and answer.

What is the pink monster doing?

It is playing computer games.

p. 70

p. 73

I want that game!

6

Tom is watching television at home this evening.
Three other children, Sue, Lucy and Bill, are watching
TV in their homes too.

The four children have a lot of computer games BUT ...
'I want that game!' they all say to their parents.

44

Tom's father has a helicopter. In the morning, Tom says,

'Please fly me to Computer Fun in Candy Street, Dad!

I want that game!'

'OK,' Tom's father says. 'Jump in!'

Sue's sister is getting on her motorbike.

'Can you take me to Computer Fun in Candy Street, please?

I want that game!' she says.

'OK!' says Sue's sister.

Lucy runs to the bus.
'Can you drive me to
Computer Fun in Candy
Street?' she asks.
'I want that game!'
'OK!' says the bus driver.
Bill phones his aunt.
'Can you take me to
Computer Fun in Candy
Street in your lorry?' he asks.
'I want that game!'
'OK,' says his aunt.

Sue, Tom, Lucy and Bill
are in the store now.
'We've only got ONE game
now,' says the man in the store.
'I want it!' says Sue.
'Me too!' says Tom.
'So do I!' says Lucy.

'And me!' says Bill.
He takes the game.
'It's mine now!' he says.

One little girl is crying. 'My friends have got a lot of computer games. But I have no computer games. Can I have that game, please?'
Bill looks at the little girl.
Sue, Tom and Lucy look at her too.

'Yes!' says Sue. 'Don't cry.' Then Sue looks at Tom.
'Yes!' says Tom.

Don't worry.

Then Tom looks at Lucy. 'Yes!' says Lucy. 'Don't be sad.' Then Lucy looks at Bill. Bill smiles and gives the game to the little girl. 'Here you are!' he says. 'It's not ours. It's yours now. Have fun!'

The little girl is really happy. 'Thanks!' she says. Sue, Tom, Lucy and Bill are happy too.

6

I want that game!

A Look and write.

a s <u>treet</u>   a b _ _   a h _ _ _ _ _ _ _ _   a l _ _ _ _   a m _ _ _ _ _ _ _ _

B Look, read and write.

1. The four children's names are ....Tom........ , Sue, Lucy and Bill.
2. The store is called Computer ....
3. Tom's .... flies him to the store.
4. The store is in .... Street.
5. .... goes to the store on a bus.
6. .... gives the game to the little girl.

C Who says this? Draw lines.

a — Sue

c — Tom

1 Don't be sad.

2 It's yours. Have fun!

3 Don't worry.

4 Don't cry.

b — Lucy

d — Bill

D Write numbers 2-6 in the boxes.

Sue: No, it isn't mine. There is Nick. Is it his?

Lucy / Jake: No, it isn't our game. Here is Anna. Is it hers?

Anna: No. There's Tom and Bill. Is it theirs?

Tom / Bill: Yes, it's ours! And it's really great!

Mark `1`: Hi, Sue. Is this computer game yours?

Nick: No, it isn't. Look! There are Lucy and Jake. Is it theirs?

Whose computer game is it? It's ....

E Look and read. Put a tick (✔) or a cross (✗) in the box.

Examples

This is a board game. ✔

These are lorries. ✗

Questions

1 This is a tablet. ☐

2 This is a plane. ☐

3 These are ears. ☐

4 These are polar bears. ☐

5 This is a sofa. ☐

F ▶ Listen and tick (✔) the box.
17

Example Which toy is the baby picking up now?

1 What is Tom drawing?

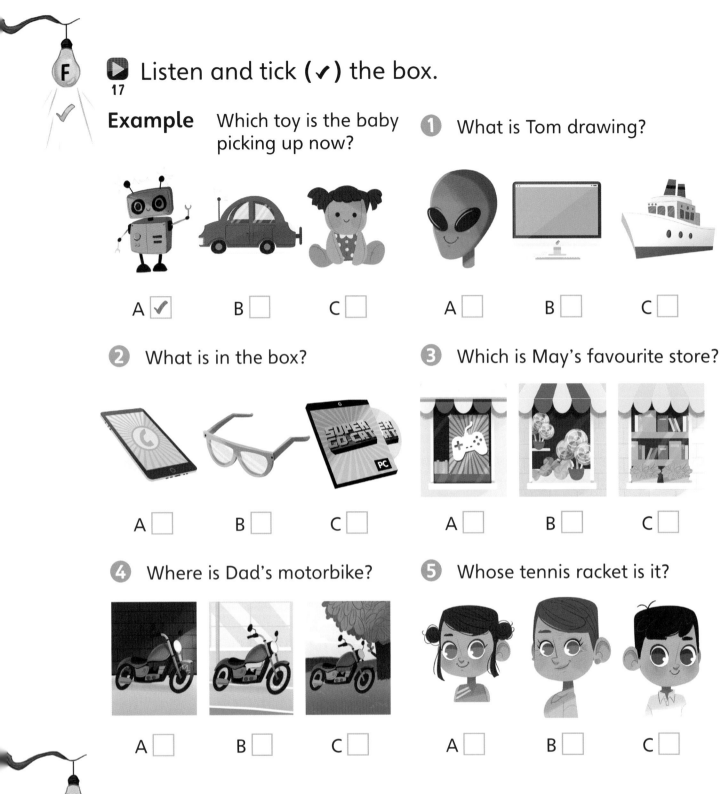

A ✔   B ☐   C ☐   A ☐   B ☐   C ☐

2 What is in the box?

3 Which is May's favourite store?

A ☐   B ☐   C ☐   A ☐   B ☐   C ☐

4 Where is Dad's motorbike?

5 Whose tennis racket is it?

A ☐   B ☐   C ☐   A ☐   B ☐   C ☐

G Look, write and say.

I can see a ....
.... and a ....

H Look and draw lines.

mouse

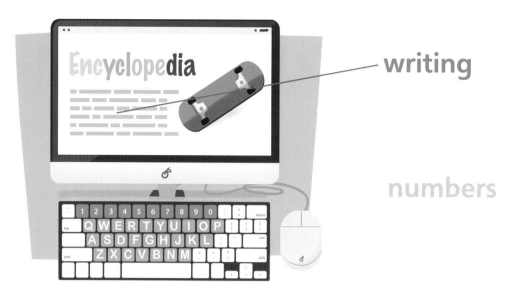

writing

keyboard

numbers

computer

letters

I ▶ Listen and sing the song.
18

Can you fly a ship?

Don't be silly! No!

Can you fly your

1 .... ?

Yes! Yes!

Can you ride on a car?

Don't be silly! No! No!

Can you ride on your sister's

2 .... ?

Yes! Yes!

Can you drive a bus?

Don't be silly! No!

Can you sit in your dad's

3 .... ?

Yes! Yes!

Can you stand on a bike?

Don't be silly! No! No!

Can you stand on your

4 .... ?

Yes! Yes!

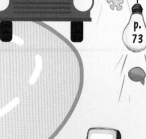

p. 70

p. 73

51

Monkey beach

Eva lives next to Monkey Beach.

She's sitting on the sand there today.

She has some lime juice to drink.

She has a kiwi and some mangoes to eat.

She has her guitar to play and her tablet too.

Eva's singing a song. She waves to Miss Board.

'Hello, Eva!' says Miss Board. 'Are you having fun?'

'Yes, I am, thanks!'

'Good! Is that a monkey behind you?'

'A monkey?' says Eva. 'No! Bye, Miss Board!'

Eva's taking photos now.

She sees Mr Page.

'Hi, Eva!' says Mr Page.

'You've got a very happy smile on your face!'

'Yes, I have. Well, it's a beautiful day!'

'Yes, it is, Eva! There's a monkey behind you! Do you know that?'

'A monkey? Behind me? Ha ha!' says Eva. 'Goodbye, Mr Page!'

Eva's hitting her ball with her new bat now.

Eva smiles at Mrs Short.

'Good morning, Eva!' says Mrs Short. 'How are you?'

'Really great, thank you!'

'Fantastic! Have you got a pet monkey now, then?'

'A pet monkey? No, I haven't!' answers Eva.

'See you, Mrs Short!'

Eva's sitting on the sand again, now.

'Right! Where's my tablet?' she says.

'Oh! There it is!
Hi, Mr Monkey!' Eva says.
The monkey smiles and gives
Eva her tablet and a coconut!
'My tablet and a coconut?
For me? Thank you,' Eva says
and claps her hands.

Sing a happy song.
Be happy! Be happy!

'Enjoy your fruit, Mr Monkey, and enjoy my song too,'
Eva laughs.

7 Monkey beach

A Look and write. Then draw lines.

k _i_ w _i_

l _ m _

c _ c _ n _ t

m _ ng _

s _ nd

B Look and read. Choose the correct word.

1. Eva has some (lime)/ **lemon** / **orange** juice.
2. Eva takes her **radio** / **tablet** / **ruler** to the beach.
3. Miss Board sees a monkey **between** / **under** / **behind** Eva.
4. Eva says it's a **beautiful** / **cool** / **fantastic** day.
5. The monkey gives Eva a **chicken** / **coconut** / **carrot**.
6. Eva **claps** / **counts** / **cleans** her hands.

C ▶ Listen and sing the song.
20

Be happy!

Sing a happy song! Be happy! Be happy!

Now clap your hands. Be happy! Be happy!

Jump and smile and sing my song!

We have a happy song to sing!

Be happy! Be happy!

D Look and write.

I have a happy song to sing.

1 Miss / book / to / funny / a / has / read. / Board

....

2 Page / to / game / Mr / has / play. / new / a

....

3 has / Mrs / hat / Short / wear. / old / to / an

....

E ▶ Listen and draw lines.
21

Alice   **Dan**   **Jill**   **Matt**

Nick   **Lucy**   **Hugo**

F Look at the pictures. Look at the letters.
Write the words.

Example

   _egg_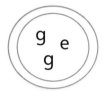

g   e
g

Questions

1    _ _ _ _

i   c
r   e

2    _ _ _ _ _ _

s   a
e   p
r   g

3    _ _ _ _ _ _

r   b   r
u   e   g

4    _ _ _ _ _ _

o   a
m   o
t   t

5   _ _ _ _ _ _ _ _

l   a   m
n   o   e
e   d

G ▶ Listen and number the pictures.
22

a    **b**    **c**    **d**  `1`

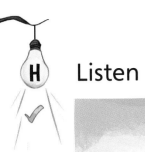

H Listen to your teacher and point. Then draw lines.

 I Write and say.

🎵 Sue's singing songs and sitting in the sea with her six sea shells!

Eva's enjoying ....
and eating ....

Dan's drawing ....
and drinking ....

Lucy's learning ....
and listening ....

p. 71
p. 73

Winners!

Hi! My name's Alex and these are my four friends.
We're in a basketball team.

I can't catch the ball,

but I'm very good at throwing.

Jill can't throw or jump, but she can run very fast!

Kim and Jim can't run fast,

but they're very good at catching.

Tom is good at bouncing, catching, throwing, jumping

and running too!

We're The Five Stars! We're really cool!

Today, we're playing basketball with The Five Suns.
They're fantastic! Alice, Dan and Sam can run very fast.
And Matt and Pat are very tall. Watch them go!
Oh, wow! They can really throw that ball!

Right! Let's start this game! We're running and jumping
and bouncing and watching. We're stopping and starting.
We're throwing and catching.

What's the score?
Oh no! We've got three
and they've got four.

'Throw it to Kim!' Jill says.
'Run, run!' Jim says.
'Catch!' Kim says to me.
'Now bounce it, bounce it
and run, run, run!
Oh, well done!
It's in the net!'

What's the score now?

Hooray! We've got five and they've got four.

We're the winners!

Now our team is smiling.

Can you jump and run fast too?

The Five Stars are very happy now.

We're all winners.

So are you!

Winners!

A Look, read and write.

smiling **bouncing** ~~playing~~
catching **starting**

1. We love ......playing...... basketball.
2. The game is .... now! Look! Wow!
3. I am throwing the ball to you and you are .... it in your hands.
4. I am .... the ball on the floor.
5. I am very, very happy! Look at my face! I am ....

B Look, read and write.

1. What is the name of Alex's team?   ..The Five Stars..
2. What game are they playing?   ....
3. What is the name of Alice's team?   ....
4. Which two children are very tall?   ....
5. Who is good at running in Alice's team? ....
6. What is the score at the end of the game? ....

C Who is good at this? Put a tick (✔) in the box.

> We're all winners.

	catching	bouncing	jumping	throwing	running
Alex				✔	
Jill					
Kim					
Jim					
Tom					

D Look and read. Write *yes* or *no*.

Examples

You can see five children.	.........yes.........
The kite is red and yellow.	..........no.........

Questions

1 The boy in green trousers is running. ....

2 A cat is playing with a ball. ....

3 One girl is wearing a blue T-shirt. ....

4 Three children are wearing hats. ....

5 The dog is brown and white. ....

E Look at the pictures and read the questions.
Write one-word answers.

Examples

What is the boy riding?   a ....bike........
What colour are his shorts?   ......white.......

1 What is in front of the boy?   a ....

2 Who is opening the door?   the ....

3 How many balls has she got?   ....

4 Where is the red ball now?   on the ....

5 What is the girl in the dress doing?   ....

F 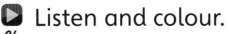 Listen and colour.

24

G Read and draw lines.

1 Are we the winners?

2 Can you run fast?

3 Where is the ball?

4 I love playing basketball!

5 Are you good at tennis?

6 We are going now.

a It is under the chair.

b So do I!

c Yes, you are. Well done!

d No, I am not!

e Oh, OK. Bye!

f Yes, I can!

H 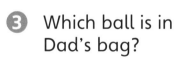 Listen and tick (✔) the box.
25

1 What is Alex doing now?

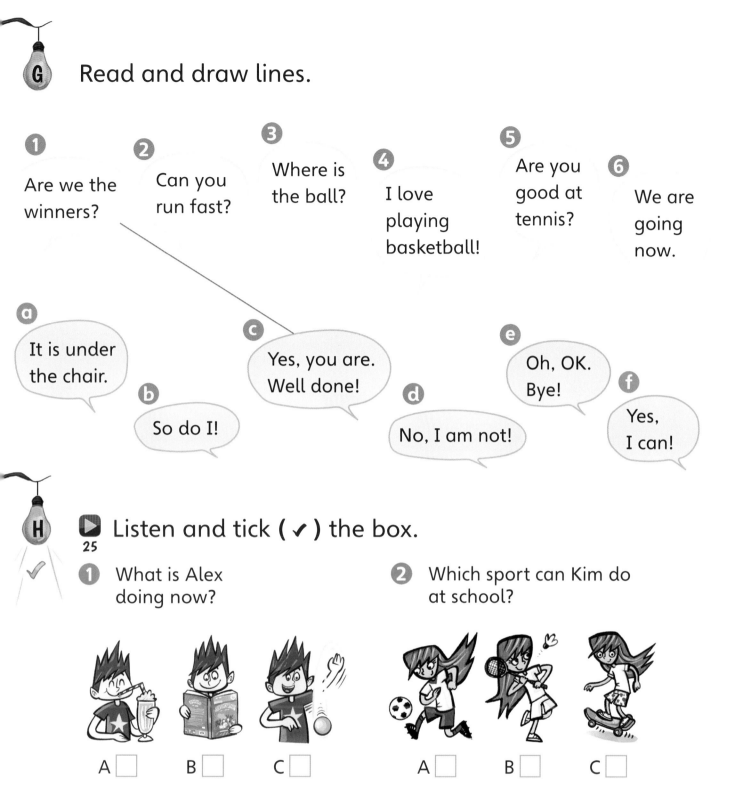

A ☐ B ☐ C ☐

2 Which sport can Kim do at school?

A ☐ B ☐ C ☐

3 Which ball is in Dad's bag?

A ☐ B ☐ C ☐

4 Who is Anna swimming with today?

A ☐ B ☐ C ☐

p. 71
p. 73

Let's have fun!

1 Design your dream bedroom.

> This is my dream bedroom. It has got … / There is …

2 Draw a funny animal.

> My animal has got a giraffe's head, a monkey's body, camel's legs and elephant's feet.

3 Make an underwater picture.

4 Make a menu.

5 Make a monster and write about it.

Our monster is ....
It is ....

It likes ....
It lives in ....

6 Make a transport poster.

Then

Now

7   Make a monkey poster.

Monkeys live in the jungle.
They eat fruit and nuts.

8   Let's throw and catch the ball. Play a game.

Let's speak!

1 **Where is it? Play a game.**

? in between   on   behind

in front of   **next to**   under

Is it under the table?

No.

Is it on the desk?

Yes.

Is it a pencil?

Yes.

2 **What is your favourite animal? Ask and answer.**

How many legs has it got?

Four legs!

Is it a horse?

Yes!

3 **What do you love doing?**

I love swimming.

Me too.

4 **On the farm. Ask and answe**

Is your farm big or small?

It's big.

What animals live there?

Cows, chickens and sheep.

5 Talk about a friend. Ask and answer.

Tell me about your friend.

She is cool!

6 What is this? Ask and answer.

What is this?

It's a ... .

7 What is in the bag? Ask and answer.

Let's put a book in the bag.

Good idea!

8 Tick (✓) the sports you can do. Find a partner.

Can you play table tennis?

Yes, I can.

Can you swim?

No, I can't

Let's say!

ee
tr**ee**

ar
guit**ar**

oo
ball**oo**n

or
st**or**y

ir
b**ir**d

er
monst**er**

ai
tr**ai**n

oa
b**oa**t

i
k**i**te

ow
c**ow**

oy
b**oy**

ear
ear

air
ch**air**

ch
chicken

j
jeans

ng
fishi**ng**

h
hippo

th
mou**th**

th
bro**th**er

z
zoo

si
televi**si**on

Wordlist

1 Our funny house

Nouns

animal
Anna
armchair
baby
balloon
bath
bathroom
bed
bedroom
bird
boat
book
bookcase
box
boy
cake
cat
chair
child
clock
colour
crocodile

cupboard
dad
desk
dining room
donkey
door
duck
elephant
face
family
flat
flower
football
fries
frog
game
garden
Grace
grandfather
grandma
grandmother
grandpa
hall
hand
hat

head
hippo
home
house
kitchen
lamp
living room
lizard
Mark
mat
mirror
mother
mum
number
orange
painting
pen
pencil
pet
piano
radio
rug
shoe
snake
sock

sofa
story
sweets
table
teeth
today
toy
tree
trousers
TV
wall
water
window
zoo

Adjectives

big
funny
green
grey
new
old
yellow

Verbs

choose
clean

come

eat

enjoy

fly

have

like

live

love

make

phone

play

see

sit

sleep

swim

walk

watch TV

wear

write

Prepositions

behind

between

in

in front of

next to

on

under

Questions

how many

what

where

which

who

whose

❷ Jill's jellyfish

Nouns

answer

bee

Ben

brother

chicken

children

cousin

cow

crayon

crocodile

dog

eraser

food

friend

giraffe

horse

jellyfish

leg

lunch

meat

mouse

mouth

Nick

polar bear

question

sea

sister

Sue

tail

teddy bear

thing

tiger

woman

zebra

Adjectives

beautiful

brown

fantastic

favourite

good

happy

little

orange

scary

small

ugly

white

young

Verbs

ask

do

find

have

learn

listen

sing

talk

try

want

Expressions

please

sorry

wow

❸ Uncle Fred and me

Nouns

afternoon

Alice

alphabet

apple

ball

beach

boot

camera

car

chocolate

class

clothes

computer

Dan

evening

Fred

guitar

hair
hockey
Hugo
jeans
kite
lake
lesson
Lucy
morning
music
name
park
Pat
person/people
picture
rain
rock
school
shell
skateboard
song
uncle
word

Adjectives

blue
cool
great
long
nice

pink
purple
red
silly

Verbs

fish
jump
read
ride a bike
run
spell
take photos
watch

④ *Mrs Day's garden*

Nouns

bag
baseball cap
bean
breakfast
bus
day
dinner
dress
egg
farm
farmer
gate
goat
onion

pea
pear
phone
potato
sheep
shirt
shop
skirt
sweater
town
truck
T-shirt
year

Adjectives

angry
dirty
gray

Verbs

count
draw
drive
open
show
tell

⑤ *Classmates*

Nouns

baseball
bread
chips

classmate
classroom
crayon
fish
hobby
juice
jungle
letter
meatball
monster
paint
paper
plane
Sam
soccer
sport
star
sun
tablet
teacher
tennis

Verbs

drink
go home
have lunch
paint
put
throw
wave

whisper

Expressions

I don't

me too

so do I

6 I want that game!

Nouns

alien

aunt

Bill

board game

bookshop

candy

computer

game

doll

driver

ear

father

fun

girl

glasses

helicopter

Jake

keyboard

lorry

man

May

motorbike

mouse

parents

racket

robot

ship

store

street

television

Tom

Adjectives

sad

Verbs

can

cry

give

know

look

pick up

ride

say

smile

stand

take

Expressions

don't worry

thanks

7 Monkey beach

Nouns

bat

board

burger

carrot

coconut

Eva

fruit

grape

jacket

kiwi

lemon

lemonade

lime

mango

monkey

night

page

pineapple

rice

sand

tomato

wave

Adjectives

short

Verbs

answer

clap

have fun

hit

kick

laugh

Expressions

hello

8 Winners!

Nouns

Alex

badminton

basketball

drink

end

floor

foot

Jim

Kim

score

shorts

team

winner

Adjectives

black

tall

Adverbs

fast

Verbs

bounce

catch

start

stop

Expressions

hooray

well done

Acknowledgements

The author would like to acknowledge the shared professionalism and FUN she's experienced whilst working with colleagues during 20 years of production of YLE tests. She would also like to thank CUP for their support in the writing of this second edition of Storyfun.

On a personal note, Karen fondly thanks her inspirational story-telling grandfather, and now, three generations later, her sons, Tom and Will, for adding so much creative fun to our continuation of the family story-telling and story-making tradition.

The author and publishers would like to thank the following ELT professionals who commented on the material at different stages of development: Louise Manicolo, Mexico; Mandy Watkins, Greece.

Design and typeset by Wild Apple Design.

Cover design and header artwork by Nicholas Jackson (Astound).

Audio production by Hart McLeod, Cambridge.

Music by Mark Fishlock and produced by Ian Harker. Recorded at The Soundhouse Studios, London.

The authors and publishers acknowledge the following sources of copyright material and are grateful for the permissions granted. While every effort has been made, it has not always been possible to identify the sources of all the material used, or to trace all copyright holders. If any omissions are brought to our notice, we will be happy to include the appropriate acknowledgements on reprinting and in the next update to the digital edition, as applicable.

Key: L = Left, R = Right, T = Top.

p. 68 (lamp): Jason Hindley/The Image Bank/Getty Images; p. 68 (wardrobe): Laara Cerman/Leigh Righton/Photolibrary/Getty Images; p. 68 (bedroom): alkir/iStock/Getty Images Plus/Getty Images; p. 70 (T): OnlyZoia/Shutterstock; p. 70 (L: car): BillPhilpot/iStock/Getty Images Plus/Getty Images; p. 70 (L: bus): Angelika Stern/E+/Getty Images; p. 70 (L: ship): AlexanderCher/iStock/Getty Images Plus/Getty Images; p. 70 (R: car): mevans/E+/Getty Images; p. 70 (R: bus): kamski/iStock/Getty Images Plus/Getty Images; p. 70 (R: ship): Mike_Kiev/iStock/Getty Images Plus/Getty Images; p. 71 (R: photo 1): Fat (Adam) Tony (Taylor)/Getty Images; p. 71 (L: photo 1): Ger Bosma/Moment Open/ Getty Images; p. 71 (L: photo 2): Nick Dale/Design Pics/Getty Images; p. 72 (photo 1): Lokibaho/ iStock/Getty Images Plus/Getty Images; p. 72 (photo 2): fstop123/E+/Getty Images; p. 72 (photo 3): Branimir76/iStock/Getty Images Plus/Getty Images; p. 72 (photo 4): skynesher/E+/Getty Images; p. 73 (photo 1): Susan Chiang/iStock/Getty Images Plus/Getty Images; p. 73 (photo 2): Asia Images/ Asia Images/Getty Images; p. 73 (photo 3): BraunS/E+/Getty Images; p. 73 (photo 4): Christopher Robbins/Iconica/Getty Images.

The authors and publishers are grateful to the following illustrators:

Judy Brown (Beehive) pp. 4, 5, 6, 7, 8, 9, 10, 11; Gaby Murphy (Advocate) pp. 12, 13, 14, 15, 16, 17, 18, 19; David Banks pp. 20, 21, 22, 23, 24, 25, 26, 27; Pip Sampson (Graham-Cameron Illustration) pp. 28, 29, 30, 31, 32, 33, 34, 35; Kelly Kennedy (Sylvie Poggio) pp. 36, 37, 38, 39, 40, 41, 42, 43; Chabe Escalante pp. 44, 45, 46, 47, 48, 49, 50, 51; pp.49 Pablo Gallego (Beehive) (Activity D: TR, ML, BL, BR) Javier Montiel pp. 52, 53, 54, 55, 56, 57, 58, 59; Melanie Sharp (Sylvie Poggio) pp. 60, 61, 62, 63, 64, 65, 66, 67.